NIGHT BEFORE COOKERY

Anne Marshall

CHARTWELL
BOOKS INC.

The Editor and the Publishers acknowledge and sincerely thank the following for their kind assistance in the preparation of this book. *New Idea* magazine for the frontispiece colour photograph of Boeuf Bourguignonne and Strawberry Flan; Casa Pupo Shop, David Jones Pty. Ltd., Sydney for china ware; Cost Less, Double Bay, Sydney for copper and brassware; Incorporated Agencies Pty. Ltd., Sydney for china, cutlery, enamel ware and glassware; New Theme Pty. Ltd., Sydney for French pottery ware; Opus, Oxford Street, Sydney for cast iron ware and glassware; Rosenthall Studio-Line, Sydney for glassware; The Bay Tree, Woollahra, Sydney for cast iron ware, English pottery and French porcelain china ware.
My sincere thanks also for help and advice go to ABC radio and *New Idea* magazine for allowing me to reproduce recipes which I have previously featured in my weekly programmes, to Norman Nicholls, a most understanding photographer, and to my assistants Anna-Marie and Jean.

This edition first published in the USA 1977 by
Chartwell Books, Inc.
A division of Book Sales, Inc.
110 Enterprise Avenue
Secaucus, New Jersey 07094

Copyright © 1977 Octopus Books Ltd

ISBN 0 7064 0643 5

Produced and printed in Hong Kong by
Mandarin Publishers Limited
22A Westlands Road, Quarry Bay, Hong Kong.

Contents

Weights and Measures

Measurements are given in cups, tablespoons and teaspoons as well as pounds and ounces.

1 standard measuring cup 8 fl oz
1 standard measuring tablespoon 20 ml
1 standard measuring teaspoon 5 ml

All measurements given are level.
To level a cup measure of solid ingredients, shake the cup gently and check the measurements at eye level.
For an accurate spoon measure, level the ingredients off with the back of a palette, French or kitchen knife or with the back of a spatula.

Note In Australia and Britain 2½ cups liquid = 20 fl oz = 1 pint

To avoid confusion all liquid measurements used in the recipes in this book are given in the Australian and British Imperial pint with the equivalent in the Australian, 8 fluid ounce cup.

Oven Temperature Guide

Description of Oven	Automatic Electric °F.	Gas °F.	Gas Regulo
Cool	200	200	0 – ½
Very Slow	250	250	½ – 1
Slow	300–325	300	1 – 2
Moderately Slow	325–350	325	2 – 3
Moderate	300–375	350	4
Moderately Hot	375–400	375	5
Hot	400–450	400	6 – 7
Very Hot	450–500	450	8 – 9

Oranges in Kirsch

Introduction

Night Before Cookery is a collection of recipes which can be made the night before they are to be served, thus saving time and avoiding fuss and bother when you are entertaining or simply catering for the family. The recipes cover first courses, soups, entrées, main courses, desserts and puddings.

The first course recipes include pâtés and terrines, many of which can be made several days ahead of serving.

Other first course dishes are egg, fish and vegetable dishes which may be prepared the night before.

Soups are a great standby for hungry children and unexpected visitors. I have included lots of my favourite recipes for nourishing, peasant-type broths like bortsch and minestrone that are a meal in themselves. There are also some dinner party soups, including a few chilled ones for summertime.

Under pastas, you will find the traditional lasagne and cannelloni — ideal dishes for heating up the next day — plus some of my favourite sauces which may be served with freshly cooked pasta. Flans, both savoury and sweet, may be prepared the night before. Savoury flans are cooked with their filling and may be reheated the next day; the sweet ones are baked 'blind' or empty and filled just before serving.

Meat pies have been family favourites for years. These are partly baked the night before and finished off just before serving. Casseroles immediately come to most people's minds when talking of night before cookery. Indeed their flavour develops and becomes much richer when left to stand overnight.

Try the basic casserole recipes for beef, lamb and pork and all their variations, or you may prefer one of the more classical casseroles or a curry.

In Desserts and Puddings, there are rich refrigerator desserts and ices for special occasions; fruits in wine and spirits, full of flavour, and ideal for formal dinner parties; fruit pies and cobblers for hungry families; more mouth-watering fruit flans; petit fours — ideal to serve at a buffet party.

I have given special tips on how to store all the dishes overnight so follow this advice carefully and you will be delighted with the results when you serve the next day.

10

Menu Planner

FAMILY DINNER
American Pork Casserole
Potatoes and Carrots
Peach Cobbler

FAMILY DINNER
Italian Lamb Casserole
Noodles and Silverbeet
Dutch Apple Flan

WEEKEND LUNCH 1
Minestrone
Speedy Spiced Pâté
Wholemeal Bread

WEEKEND LUNCH 2
Italian Fish Soup
Tomato Flan
Green Salad

SATURDAY SUPPER
Spaghetti Bolognaise
Green Salad
Gooseberry Fool

SUNDAY SUPPER
English Beef Casserole
Jacket Baked Potatoes
Cherry Compote

FORMAL DINNER PARTY 1
Nova Scotia Eggs
Swiss Veal
French Apricot Tart

FORMAL DINNER PARTY 2
Cold Tomato Soup
Coq au Vin
Charlotte Malakhov

BUFFET DINNER PARTY 1
Simple Terrine
Boeuf Bourguignonne
Strawberry Flan

BUFFET DINNER PARTY 2
Lamb Curry
Chicken Curry
Liqueur Rum Truffles

DINNER FOR FOUR 1
Green Pea Soup
Chicken Pie
Orange Water Ice

DINNER FOR FOUR 2
Ratatouille
Blanquette of Veal
Blackberry and Apple Pie

Pâtés and Terrines

Speedy Spiced Pâté

Serves 6 - 8

8 oz liverwurst
4 oz cream cheese
2 tablespoons mayonnaise
3 tablespoons cream
1 teaspoon Worcestershire sauce
½ teaspoon curry powder
1 teaspoon brandy or dry vermouth
salt and pepper

Mix liverwurst and cream cheese with mayonnaise, cream,
Worcestershire sauce, curry powder and brandy until
smoothly combined. Add salt and pepper to taste. Place in
a pâté mould lined with aluminium foil, or in individual
pots, cover with clear plastic wrap or aluminium foil and
chill until required.
Serve in individual pots, or turn out of mould and serve in
slices on individual plates accompanied by slices of
freshly-made, hot, crisp toast. This pâté is also delicious
for a 'help-yourself' lunch, served with black rye bread or
crispbread, pickles or salad and a glass of wine.
*Storage tip: Store pâté, well covered, with plastic wrap or
aluminium foil, in refrigerator until required for serving.*

Speedy spiced pâté

Chicken Liver Pâté

Serves 8

Cooking time: 10 minutes

2 onions, finely chopped
2 cloves garlic, crushed
6 oz butter or margarine
1 lb chicken livers, trimmed
1 tablespoon finely chopped parsley
1 bay leaf
pinch of thyme
salt and pepper
1 tablespoon brandy
radishes and fresh dry toast for serving

Lightly fry onion and garlic in 4 oz butter or margarine until soft. Add chicken livers and cook for a further 2-3 minutes. Add chopped parsley, bay leaf, thyme, salt and pepper. Cook for a further 2 minutes. Remove bay leaf. Cool and pound all the ingredients well together, using a wooden potato masher or a wooden spoon, or purée the mixture in an electric blender. Melt remaining fat and add together with brandy. Pack into a pâté mould, or a small loaf tin, lined with a strip of aluminium foil, and chill thoroughly, covered with plastic wrap or aluminium foil.
Turn out and serve garnished with crisp radishes and accompanied with thin slices of fresh, hot, crisp toast or slices of fresh French bread. This pâté is delicious, easy to make and suitable for serving as a first course.
Variations: Duck livers or calf's liver may be used in place of chicken livers.
Storage tip: Chill the pâté, well-covered with foil or plastic wrap, overnight, in a pâté mould or loaf tin, as directed in recipe. Serve from the refrigerator whenever required. It keeps for several days stored this way.

Chopped Chicken Livers

Serves 8

Cooking time: 10 minutes

1 lb chicken livers
1 onion, finely chopped
2 oz (2 tablespoons) chicken fat
2 hard-boiled eggs
1 stalk celery, finely chopped (optional)
salt and pepper

Prepare the chicken livers, remove threads and tubes. Gently fry onion in the heated chicken fat until soft. Add chicken livers and lightly fry (2-3 minutes). Chop hard-boiled eggs coarsely, retaining 1 egg yolk for garnish. Mince the onion and chicken liver, mix with chopped hard-boiled egg and chopped celery, if used, or chop chicken liver and mix well with other ingredients in a bowl. Season to taste with salt and pepper and mix well.

Shape the mixture into eight rounds on eight small individual plates and sprinkle with sieved egg yolk. Alternatively, serve individual portions on a lettuce leaf on eight individual plates and garnish with sieved egg yolk.

This is a traditional Jewish dish which is served as a first course. It is eaten with a small knife and fork. Chicken fat may be purchased at leading delicatessen stores.

Storage tip: Cover individual plates (without lettuce) with clear plastic wrap and refrigerate overnight until ready to serve. Alternatively, all the mixture may be covered tightly in a bowl or plastic container and refrigerated overnight, then placed on individual plates just before serving.

Terrine Maison

Serves 12

Cooking time: 2 hours

Oven temperature: 325-350° F

8 oz thin streaky bacon rashers
8 oz lean veal, minced (ground)
8 oz pork, minced (ground)
8 oz pig's, calf's or lamb's liver, minced (ground)
2 oz (2 tablespoons) butter or margarine
6 shallots (spring onions) or 1 small onion, finely chopped
1 clove garlic, finely chopped
4-8 oz chicken livers
2 tablespoons brandy
1 tablespoon lemon juice
1 tablespoon chopped fresh herbs or 1 teaspoon dried herbs
1 egg
2 tablespoons cream (optional)
salt and freshly ground black pepper
1 bay leaf

Line a terrine or straight-sided casserole with overlapping rinded rashers of bacon. The bacon may hang over the side and be folded back over the top later.
Mix the minced veal, pork and liver together in a mixing bowl. Heat butter in a small frying pan and gently fry shallots and garlic until soft but not brown, drain and add to meat. Fry the whole chicken livers for 2-3 minutes. Put chicken livers on a plate and leave to cool.
Add brandy and lemon juice to frying pan, stir over a low heat to loosen sediment and add to meat. Add herbs, beaten egg, cream if used, salt and pepper. Mix meat mixture until all ingredients are well blended. Place half mixture into the terrine, press down firmly and smooth the top. Cut chicken livers into quarters and place in a row down centre of the meat. Cover with remaining meat mixture, smooth top, cover with bacon rashers and place a bay leaf on top.
Cover with foil then with a tight fitting lid. Place in a bain marie as for Simple Terrine (page 19) and bake in the centre of a moderately slow oven for 2 hours. Cool and press as for Simple Terrine. Turn out or serve slices from the mould.
Storage tip: See Simple Terrine.

Terrine maison

Christmas Pâté

Serves 4

8 oz cooked goose or turkey
4 oz butter or margarine
1 tablespoon dry sherry
pinch of ground cloves
pinch of black pepper
½ teaspoon salt
½ teaspoon lemon juice
2 drops Tabasco sauce
2 oz extra butter or margarine, melted

Mince 8 oz leftover Christmas goose or turkey. Chop the meat finely if you do not have a mincer. Cream butter or margarine well and beat in the minced poultry meat, sherry, cloves, pepper, salt, lemon juice and Tabasco sauce. Place mixture into individual pots, smooth top and pour melted butter or margarine over top of each. Cover with clear plastic wrap or aluminium foil and chill in refrigerator. Serve with fingers of freshly-made, hot, crisp toast.

This is a good way to use up leftovers from the Christmas bird.

Storage tip: Store in refrigerator, covered with clear plastic wrap or aluminium foil, until ready to serve. Pâté which is potted and covered with a layer of melted fat will keep for a few days if stored in a cool dry place in a cold climate. The alcohol in the recipe acts as a preservative for a while as well as adding flavour to the pâté.

Simple Terrine

Serves 12

Cooking time: 1-1½ hours

Oven temperature: 325-350°F

1 lb mixed pork and veal, minced
8 oz sausage meat
8 oz pig's or lamb's liver, minced
1 onion, finely chopped
1 tablespoon chopped fresh herbs or 1 teaspoon dried herbs
1 cup fresh breadcrumbs
1 egg
salt and pepper
8 oz thin streaky bacon rashers
1 bay leaf

Mix veal and pork mince thoroughly with sausage meat, minced liver, chopped onion and herbs, breadcrumbs, beaten egg and salt and pepper.

Line a terrine or straight-sided ovenproof casserole with overlapping rinded bacon rashers. Fill the terrine with the meat mixture, press down firmly into the corners and smooth the surface. Cover with more bacon rashers and place a bay leaf on top. Cover with a piece of aluminium foil and lid of casserole.

Place in a roasting pan and add boiling water to come half way up the pan to make a bain marie. Place in the middle of a moderately slow oven and cook for 1-1½ hours or until firm to the touch.

Remove from bain marie, remove lid and foil and cover with a piece of clean foil and press with a heavy weight until cold. Turn terrine out and serve in thick slices with brown bread or freshly-made crisp toast.

Storage tip: Store cold terrine in its dish in refrigerator until ready to serve. It keeps in the refrigerator for several days.

More Night Before
First Courses

Nova Scotia Eggs

Serves 8

Cooking time: 5 minutes

8 thin slices smoked salmon
juice of 1 large lemon
8 coddled eggs
16 tablespoons (approx. 2 cups) mayonnaise
shredded lettuce and lemon slices for garnish

Lay a slice of smoked salmon carefully onto the centre of
eight small individual plates and sprinkle with lemon juice.
Place a coddled egg onto the centre of each slice of smoked
salmon. Coat each egg neatly with 2 tablespoons thick
mayonnaise. Cover plates individually with plastic wrap and
refrigerate until ready to serve. Serve with shredded lettuce
around each egg and garnish with a thin slice or segment of
lemon.
To coddle eggs: Place the eggs gently in a pan of boiling water
and boil gently for 5 minutes. Plunge into a bowl of cold
water immediately. When cold, remove shell carefully.
Storage tip: Place prepared eggs (without lettuce and garnish)
covered individually, with plastic wrap, in refrigerator
overnight. Coddled eggs do not dry out as much as hard-boiled
eggs when stored in the refrigerator.

Tuna Mornay Scallops

Serves 6-8

Cooking time: 20-25 minutes

Oven temperature: 350-375°F

1 medium can (approx. 8 oz) tuna
finely grated rind and juice of 1 lemon
1 tablespoon chopped parsley
¾ pint (approx. 2 cups) white sauce
2 oz Cheddar cheese, grated
salt
pinch of cayenne pepper
½ cup buttered breadcrumbs
lemon segments and parsley sprigs for garnish

Drain tuna, flake with a fork and place into six or eight
scallop dishes or shells. Sprinkle with lemon rind, lemon
juice and chopped parsley. Make white sauce and stir in
grated cheese over a medium heat until cheese melts.
Season to taste with salt and cayenne pepper. Pour sauce
evenly over tuna and sprinkle with breadcrumbs. Cool,
cover with clear plastic wrap or aluminium foil and
refrigerate overnight.
To finish and serve, remove plastic wrap or foil, stand on a
baking tray and place in moderate oven for 15-20 minutes
or until heated through. Serve hot, standing on a small plate
garnished with lemon and parsley sprigs.
To make white sauce: Melt 1½ oz (1½ tablespoons) butter
or margarine in a saucepan. Add 1½ oz (3 tablespoons)
plain flour and stir over a medium heat for 1 minute. Add
¾ pint (2 cups) milk and bring to the boil, stirring
continuously, until the sauce thickens.
To make buttered breadcrumbs: Fry 1 cup fresh breadcrumbs
in 2 oz (2 tablespoons) butter or margarine, stirring
continuously, until golden brown and fairly crisp.
*Storage tip: Store in refrigerator overnight as directed in
recipe. These should not be stored for longer than 24 hours
and do not freeze well.*

Ratatouille

Serves 8

Cooking time: 45 minutes

Oven temperature: 350-375°F

5 tablespoons olive oil
2 onions, thinly sliced
2 cloves garlic, thinly sliced
4 zucchini (courgettes), sliced
1 green pepper, seeded and sliced
1 small eggplant (aubergine), peeled, diced and degorged
1 tablespoon chopped fresh basil or 1 teaspoon dried basil
4 tomatoes, coarsely chopped
1 teaspoon salt
¼ teaspoon pepper

Heat oil in a flameproof casserole or pan and fry onions
until soft and golden. Add garlic, zucchini and green pepper,
cover and cook over a fairly high heat for 5 minutes. Add
eggplant, basil, tomatoes, salt and pepper. Cover casserole
or pan and continue cooking for 20-30 minutes, until
vegetables are tender but not mushy. If using a casserole
you may transfer the Ratatouille to a moderate oven to
cook, if using a pan, simmer gently over a low heat.
Serve Ratatouille slightly chilled on small individual
plates as an hors d'oeuvre.
To degorge eggplant means to sprinkle cut eggplant with
salt and leave for 30 minutes - this makes the excess
liquid ooze out. Drain the degorged eggplant before
cooking.
Variation: Serve Ratatouille hot as mixed vegetables to
accompany grilled or fried meat.
*Storage tip: Cool Ratatouille, cover with a tight fitting
lid, aluminium foil or plastic wrap and store in refrigerator
until ready to serve. It keeps for several days stored in this
manner.*

Sweet Corn Scallops

Serves 6-8

Cooking time: 25-30 minutes

Oven temperature: 350-375° F

1 x 10 oz packet frozen sweet corn
¾ pint (approx. 2 cups) white sauce
2 tablespoons cream
salt
pinch each of cayenne pepper and nutmeg
½ cup buttered breadcrumbs
3 rashers bacon
parsley sprigs for garnish

Cook sweet corn according to directions on packet, drain
well. Make white sauce (see Tuna Mornay Scallops, page 22)
add cream and season to taste with salt, cayenne pepper
and nutmeg. Stir in sweet corn, divide between six or
eight scallop dishes or shells and sprinkle with buttered
breadcrumbs (see Tuna Mornay Scallops). Cool, cover with
clear plastic wrap or aluminium foil and refrigerate overnight.
Rind bacon rashers and stretch to equal thickness by
stroking with the back of a knife. Cut each rasher into three
pieces, roll up tightly and thread onto a metal skewer. Wrap
securely in clear plastic wrap and refrigerate overnight.
To finish and serve, remove plastic wrap or foil, stand on a
baking tray and place in a moderate oven for 15-20
minutes or until heated through. Remove plastic wrap from
bacon rolls and cook under a hot grill, (broiler) turning
occasionally until cooked and crisp. Serve Sweet Corn
Scallops hot, standing on a small plate, garnished with bacon
rolls and parsley sprigs.
*Storage tip: Store in refrigerator overnight as directed in
recipe. These should not be stored for longer than 24 hours
and do not freeze well.*

Soups

Dutch Pea Soup

Serves 10-12

Cooking time: 5 hours

1 knuckle bacon
1 pig's trotter
1 lb dried green split peas
6 pints (15 cups) cold water
2 onions, chopped
2 leeks, thinly sliced (optional)
2 stalks celery, sliced
2 oz (2 tablespoons) butter or margarine
salt and pepper
4 frankfurts, sliced

A delicious cheap soup.
Ask your butcher for an unsalted knuckle of bacon and an
unsalted pig's trotter. Soak bacon in cold water overnight.
Soak pig's trotter overnight also if it is salted. Soak dried
peas for 24 hours.
Place drained dried peas and water in a large heavy-based pan,
cover, bring to the boil and simmer for 2 hours. Add the
bacon and pig's trotter and simmer for a further 2 hours.
Meanwhile, fry prepared vegetables in heated butter or
margarine in a frying pan until soft.
Allow pea soup to cool, remove meat and sieve or liquidise
in an electric blender. Return soup purée to the pan, add
fried vegetables and simmer, covered, for 1 hour, stirring
occasionally to prevent burning. Remove meat from bacon
knuckle, cut into small pieces and add to soup. Discard the
pig's trotter. Reheat soup, season to taste and add more water
if it is too thick. Add sliced frankfurts and serve soup hot.
Storage tip: Place the sieved soup with chopped meat in a
clean bowl, cover and store in refrigerator. Add frankfurts
while reheating. This soup freezes well.

Shellfish Chowder

Serves 6-8

Cooking time: 1 hour approx.

1 lb prawns or crayfish, in shell
4 oz salt pork or bacon
2 tablespoons oil or margarine
1 onion, finely chopped
1 lb new potatoes
2 tomatoes, chopped
½ pint (1¼ cups) milk
salt
freshly ground black pepper
¼ pint (⅔ cup) cream (optional)

Shell and de-vein prawns, or remove crayfish meat from shell.
Place shells in a pan with 1 pint (2½ cups) cold water, cover,
bring slowly to the boil and simmer for 15 minutes. Strain off
fish stock and make up to 1 pint. Discard fish shells. Dice
shellfish. Remove rind from salt pork and dice, (cut bacon into
½ inch strips). Fry salt pork in oil in a large heavy-based pan
until golden brown, remove from pan. Gently fry chopped
onion in pan until soft and transparent. Scrub new potatoes
and fry for 1-2 minutes. Add stock, salt pork and tomatoes,
cover and simmer for 30 minutes, or until potatoes are tender.
Add shellfish and milk, heat through gently and add salt and
pepper to taste. Stir cream in just before serving, if used. Serve
soup hot. This chowder, like all other chowders, is almost a
meal in itself.
Storage tip: Transfer soup, without cream, to another vessel,
cool quickly and store covered in refrigerator. Soups
containing salt pork or bacon do not freeze well.

Bortsch

Serves 8

Cooking time: 2 hours approx.

1 onion, thinly sliced
1 tablespoon oil or soft margarine
8 oz stewing beef (shin or chuck)
3 pints (7½ cups) cold water
2 teaspoons salt
½ teaspoon pepper
1 bay leaf
1 tablespoon chopped fresh thyme or 1 teaspoon dried thyme
1 clove garlic, finely chopped
1 carrot, thinly sliced
½ small turnip, thinly sliced
¼ cabbage, finely shredded
2 tomatoes, peeled and chopped
2 beetroot, peeled and grated
½ pint (1¼ cups) sour cream

Fry onion slowly in oil or margarine in a large heavy-based
pan until golden brown. Remove fat and coarse tissues from
beef and cut into ½ inch cubes. Add meat to pan and fry
until brown. Add cold water, salt, pepper, herbs and
garlic, cover and bring to the boil, reduce heat and simmer
gently.
Meanwhile, prepare carrot, turnip and cabbage and add to pan.
Return to the boil and simmer for 1 hour. Add tomatoes and
simmer for a further 30 minutes.
Add grated beetroot to hot soup 5 minutes before serving.
This gives it a rich ruby red colour. Taste and add more salt
and pepper if necessary. Serve hot with a heaped teaspoon of
sour cream on top of each serving of soup. Serve with rye or
sweet and sour bread.
*Storage tip: Remove soup from heat before adding beetroot.
Cool and store in refrigerator. When ready to serve, reheat,
add beetroot and simmer for 5 minutes*

Bortsch

Italian Fish Soup

Serves 6-8

Cooking time: 1 hour approx.

1 onion, thinly sliced
6 tablespoons olive oil
2 lb tomatoes
2 tablespoons chopped parsley
1 clove garlic, finely chopped
3 lb mixed white fish (flathead, bream, whiting, leatherjacket)
salt and pepper
½ cup white wine (optional)

Gently fry onion in heated olive oil in a large, heavy-based pan, until soft and transparent. Peel tomatoes and chop coarsely. Add tomatoes, parsley and garlic to pan, cover and simmer for 15 minutes.

Meanwhile, prepare fish by filleting, removing skin and cutting into bite-size pieces. Place fish skins and bones in a pan with 1 pint cold water. Cover, bring to the boil and simmer for 15 minutes. Strain off fish stock and discard bones and skin. Add fish pieces and stock to tomato mixture, cover and bring to the boil. Simmer for 10-15 minutes, or until fish is tender. Season to taste with salt and pepper. Add wine, if used, and bring soup back to a gentle simmer before serving. Serve hot, with French bread.

This recipe for fish soup is very nourishing and particularly light.

Storage tip: Place soup, without wine, into another vessel, cool quickly and store covered in refrigerator. This soup may be frozen successfully.

Italian fish soup

Green Pea Soup

Serves 6

Cooking time: 45 minutes

1 lb frozen green peas
2 oz (2 tablespoons) butter or margarine
1 tablespoon water
1 teaspoon sugar
1 teaspoon salt
¼ teaspoon pepper
1 oz (2 tablespoons) plain flour
2 pints (5 cups) chicken stock or water and chicken stock
   cubes
2 onions, finely chopped
½ pint (1¼ cups) sour cream
½ teaspoon caraway seeds

Thaw frozen peas in a colander under running cold water,
drain and place in pan. Add 1 oz butter or margarine, water,
sugar, salt and pepper and simmer until tender. Add flour
and cook for 1-2 minutes, stirring. Add chicken stock,
bring to the boil, reduce heat and simmer for 30 minutes.
Cool then sieve or mix to a puree in an electric blender.
Heat remaining butter or margarine and gently fry chopped
onion until soft and golden. Add to soup. Add sour cream
and caraway seeds, cover and simmer for 10-15 minutes.
Serve hot.
Storage tip: Place the cold soup puree after sieving or
liquidising in electric mixer into a clean bowl. Cover and store
in refrigerator. Next day or night, add fried onion, sour cream
and caraway seeds before reheating.

Minestrone

Serves 8 - 10

Cooking time: 4 hours

8 oz haricot beans
8 oz salted belly pork
1 onion, chopped
2 cloves garlic, finely chopped
4 pints (10 cups) water
4 beef stock cubes
2 carrots, thinly sliced
2 stalks celery, chopped
¼ cabbage, thinly shredded
2 tomatoes, peeled and chopped
salt and pepper
4 oz peas, fresh or frozen
4 oz green beans
4 oz macaroni
2 tablespoons chopped parsley
4 oz grated Parmesan cheese for serving

Soak haricot beans in cold water overnight (approx. 12
hours). Drain, place in a clean pan with cold water to cover
and simmer, covered, for 1½ hours. Drain well.
Remove skin from pork and cut pork into ½ inch cubes.
Place pork in a large heavy-based pan, cover and saute pork
in its own fat until brown, shaking pan occasionally. Add
chopped onion and garlic and fry until soft. Add water,
beef stock cubes, drained haricot beans, prepared carrots,
celery, cabbage, tomatoes, salt and pepper. Cover and bring
to the boil, reduce heat and simmer soup for 1½ hours.
Add peas, green beans broken into large pieces and macaroni
broken into small pieces, simmer for a further 20 minutes
or until macaroni is tender. More water may be added at
this stage if soup is too thick. Taste soup and add more salt
and pepper if necessary. Stir in chopped parsley just before
serving. Serve hot sprinkled with Parmesan cheese.
This is an Italian peasant soup. You may stir in 2 tablespoons
olive oil just before serving to make it more authentic.
*Storage tip: Cool soup and store covered in another vessel
in refrigerator. Add parsley after reheating. This soup
freezes successfully.*

Cold Tomato Soup

Serves 6-8

Cooking time: 1 hour approx.

2 lb ripe tomatoes
1 small onion, chopped
1 bay leaf
6 peppercorns
2 cloves
1 strip of lemon rind
2 pints (5 cups) chicken stock or water and chicken stock
   cubes
1 tablespoon arrowroot or cornflour
salt
freshly ground black pepper
½ cup fresh orange juice
½ cup cream and grated orange rind for garnish

Wash tomatoes, cut in two, squeeze seeds out and remove
any green stalk. Place in a pan with onion, bay leaf,
peppercorns, cloves, lemon rind and stock. Cover and bring
to the boil, reduce heat and simmer for 1 hour . Cool and
press through a sieve with a wooden spoon, or mix to a
purée in an electric blender.

Blend arrowroot with 3 tablespoons cold water, add to
tomato soup and bring to the boil, stirring continuously.
Season to taste. Add orange juice. Cool, then chill
thoroughly. Serve in chilled bowls with a little cream in
each, sprinkle a little orange rind on top.
Storage tip: Store cold soup covered in refrigerator. This
soup freezes well.

Iced Cucumber Soup

Serves 4

1 large cucumber
2 x 8 oz cartons plain yoghurt
2 teaspoons white wine vinegar
1 teaspoon olive oil
salt
cayenne pepper
1 tablespoon chopped fresh mint

34

Peel the cucumber, slice in half lengthways, remove seeds
with a teaspoon and chop cucumber coarsely. Blend
prepared cucumber and yoghurt in an electric blender
until smooth. Add vinegar and oil and stir well. Season to
taste with salt and a pinch of cayenne pepper. Place in a clean
bowl or soup tureen, cover and chill in the refrigerator.
Serve chilled in chilled soup bowls sprinkled with chopped
mint. Add an ice cube to each portion.
*Storage tip: Store covered in refrigerator, without ice cubes
until ready to serve.*

Vichyssoise

Serves 8

Cooking time: 40 minutes

4 leeks
4 oz butter or margarine
1 large white onion, finely chopped
2 pints (5 cups) chicken stock or water and chicken stock
     cubes
2 medium size potatoes, peeled and sliced
1 tablespoon chopped parsley
1 stalk celery, chopped
salt
white pepper
½ pint (1¼ cups) cream, chilled
chopped chives for garnish

Slice leeks ¼-inch thick, using white part plus about 1-inch
of lightest green leek. Melt butter in a·large heavy pan and
sauté leeks and chopped onion, covered, over a low heat
until soft (about 10 minutes). Add chicken stock, sliced
potato, parsley, celery, salt and pepper, cover and simmer
until potato is tender (about 30 minutes). Cool.
Rub soup through a sieve or mix to a purée in an electric
blender. Taste and season if necessary. Place in a large bowl or
soup tureen, cover and chill well. Just before serving, stir
in chilled cream. Serve chilled in chilled soup bowls, sprinkled
with chopped chives.
When leeks are out of season, replace with the white stalks
of shallots or spring onions.
*Storage tip: Store the cold soup, without cream, covered in
a clean container in the refrigerator. Stir cream in just
before serving as directed.*

Pasta

Tagliatelle with Bacon and Tomato Sauce

Serve 4-6

Cooking time: 20 minutes

3 oz (3 tablespoons) butter or margarine
8 oz lean back bacon, diced
1 carrot, diced
4 stalks celery, chopped
1 clove garlic, chopped
4 tablespoons tomato paste (purée)
½ cup water
1 small chicken stock cube
salt and pepper
8-12 oz tagliatelle
2 tablespoons grated Parmesan cheese

Heat 2 oz of butter or margarine and gently fry the diced
bacon for 4-5 minutes. Add prepared carrot, celery and garlic,
cover and saute for 5 minutes, shaking pan occasionally. Add
tomato paste, water, stock cube, salt and pepper. Cook gently
for a further 5 minutes.

Cook tagliatelle according to directions on the packet, usually
for 15-20 minutes in a large pan of boiling, salted water until
tender.

To serve, drain tagliatelle, return to pan, add remaining butter
or margarine and shake over heat until tagliatelle is well
coated. Add Parmesan cheese, stir in gently then transfer to
a warm serving dish. Pour the hot bacon and tomato sauce on
top and serve immediately.

Tagliatelle is a long, flat strip of pasta made from an egg
noodle dough.

*Storage tip: The bacon and tomato sauce may be made in
advance and stored in the refrigerator overnight. The
tagliatelle must be cooked freshly just before serving.*

Tagliatelle with bacon and tomato sauce

Spaghetti Bolognaise

Serves 4-6

Cooking time: 1 hour 20 minutes

2 tablespoons olive oil
2 oz (2 tablespoons) butter or margarine
2 rashers bacon, rinded and chopped
1 onion, chopped
1 carrot, finely chopped
1 clove garlic, finely chopped
8 oz finely minced beef
½ pint (1¼ cups) beef stock or water and beef stock cube
4 tablespoons tomato paste (purée)
1 bay leaf
½ teaspoon salt
freshly ground black pepper
½ cup red wine
8-12 oz spaghetti
grated Parmesan cheese for serving

Heat oil and butter in a heavy-based pan and gently fry bacon,
onion, carrot and garlic for 5 minutes. Add beef and cook,
stirring occasionally, until it turns brown (about 10 minutes).
Add stock, tomato paste, bay leaf, salt and pepper and bring
to the boil stirring frequently. Reduce heat and simmer covered
for 1 hour. Stir in wine and season to taste if necessary. Boil
spaghetti in a large pan of boiling, salted water until tender,
about 15-20 minutes. Drain well, return to pan with a
tablespoon of olive oil and shake over heat until all strands
of spaghetti are separated and coated with oil. Serve hot with
hot Bolognaise sauce, sprinkled with grated Parmesan cheese.
*Storage tip: The Bolognaise sauce may be stored covered,
overnight in the refrigerator. The sauce freezes well without
the wine. Boil spaghetti freshly just before serving as it does
not store well when cooked.*

Lasagne with Meat and Cream Sauce

Serves 6-8

Cooking time: 1½ hours

Oven temperature: 350-375°F

1 quantity Bolognaise sauce (see recipe opposite)
8 oz lasagne
Cream sauce:
1½ oz (1½ tablespoons) butter or margarine
1½ oz (3 tablespoons) plain flour
¾ pint (approx. 2 cups) milk
½ cup cream
1 teaspoon salt
¼ teaspoon white pepper
½ teaspoon ground nutmeg
2 oz grated Parmesan cheese for sprinkling

Make Bolognaise sauce as directed and simmer for 45 minutes.
Boil lasagne in a large pan of boiling, salted water until tender,
about 15-20 minutes. Stir occasionally to prevent sticking.
Add sufficient cold water to pan to cool lasagne then transfer
gently and lay on a clean teatowel to drain.
To make cream sauce: Melt butter or margarine in a saucepan,
stir in flour and cook roux over a medium heat for 1-2 minutes
stirring continuously. Add the milk and cream and bring to the
boil, stirring continuously. Reduce heat and simmer for 2
minutes. Add salt, pepper and nutmeg and remove from heat.
To finish lasagne: Spread a layer of Bolognaise sauce over
the bottom of a greased shallow 9 x 12-inch casserole or
baking dish. Cover with a layer of cream sauce. Lay
overlapping strips of lasagne on top. Repeat layers twice more
and top with another layer of Bolognaise and cream sauce.
Sprinkle with Parmesan cheese. Bake in a moderate oven for
30 minutes until bubbling hot. Serve immediately.
Quick tip: Use a quick creaming margarine for the cream
sauce, place all the ingredients in a saucepan and whisk with
a wire balloon whisk over a medium-high heat until the
sauce boils and thickens.
*Storage tip: Cover the layered lasagne with aluminium foil
or plastic wrap and refrigerate overnight. Bake the next day.*

Cannelloni with Ham and Mushrooms

Serves 4-6

Cooking time: 1 hour approx.

Oven temperature: 350-375°F

8 - 12 oz cannelloni
Filling:
8 oz mushrooms, chopped
8 oz cooked ham, diced
1 onion, chopped
2 tablespoons olive oil
1 oz (1 tablespoon) butter or margarine
2 tablespoons grated Parmesan cheese
salt
freshly ground black pepper
2 tablespoons grated Parmesan cheese for sprinkling
Cheese sauce:
1½ oz (1½ tablespoons) soft margarine
1½ oz (3 tablespoons) plain flour
¾ pint (approx. 2 cups) milk
3 tablespoons grated Parmesan cheese
salt and freshly ground black pepper

Boil cannelloni in a large pan of boiling water with 2 tablespoons salt, for 15 minutes. Stir frequently to prevent sticking. Remove with a slotted spoon and place on a clean teatowel to drain. Leave to cool.

To make filling: Sauté mushrooms, ham and onion in oil and fat until vegetables are cooked. Cool, add cheese and salt and pepper to taste. Fill the cannelloni using a teaspoon.

To make cheese sauce: Place margarine, flour and milk in a saucepan and whisk continuously over heat, with a wire balloon whisk, until the sauce boils and thickens. Add Parmesan cheese and salt and pepper to taste.

To finish cannelloni: Pour sufficient sauce into a greased shallow baking dish to cover the base. Arrange the filled cannelloni side by side in single layer in the baking dish. Cover with remaining sauce, sprinkle with remaining 2 tablespoons grated Parmesan cheese and bake in a moderate oven for 30 minutes. Serve hot. Serve two cannelloni for an entrée, three to four for a main course.
Storage tip: Cannelloni may be prepared the night before serving but it should not be baked until just before serving. Cover prepared cannelloni (unbaked) and store overnight in refrigerator.

Quiches and Flans

Basic Savoury Flan
Serves 4-6

Cooking time: 30-35 minutes

Oven temperature: 375—400°F

6 oz short crust pastry
greaseproof paper
haricot beans or similar (dried peas, rice or crusts of stale
    bread)

Roll pastry out on a lightly floured board or surface to a
round ⅛ inch thick. Lift pastry over rolling pin and unroll
into an 8 inch flan ring, standing on an open-ended baking
tray, or unroll into an 8 inch flan tin. Press pastry gently
but firmly into shape of flan tin, using the back of the
fingers, lightly floured, and working from the centre to the
edge to press out any air bubbles. Trim pastry from top
edge of flan by rolling over lightly with a rolling pin. Prick
base of flan lightly with a fork.
To bake when filled: Place filling in flan, according to choice
as directed in 'Variations' and bake towards the top of a
moderately hot oven for 30-35 minutes, or until filling is
set and pastry is cooked. Cool on a wire cooling tray if not
serving immediately from oven. Serves 6-8 as an entree, 4-6
as main course.
To bake blind: See Basic Fruit Flan recipe (page 83).
This quantity of pastry, 6 oz, is sufficient to make a 7-8 inch
flan. A good flan should have a very thin pastry casing and
can be made with 4 oz short crust pastry by practised pastry
cooks, however, I suggest you use 6 oz pastry if you are not
used to handling pastry.
*Storage tip: The finished flan may be cooled and stored
overnight in a refrigerator. Reheat in a moderate oven
(350—375°F) for 20-30 minutes to serve hot, or serve
cold. You will get a better result, however, if you*

42

refrigerate the shaped flan case (uncooked) in the flan tin or flan ring standing on a baking tray, and refrigerate the prepared filling overnight. Next day, pour prepared filling into the flan case and bake as directed. Serve freshly baked, puffed and golden from the oven. Baked flans freeze successfully in a sealed plastic bag or wrapped securely in aluminium foil.

Variations of Basic Savoury Flan

Quiche Lorraine

Place 4 oz streaky bacon, rinded, grilled and chopped, in the bottom of the uncooked pastry flan. Whisk together 2 large eggs, ¼ pint (⅝ cup) cream, 6 thinly sliced shallots (optional) and a pinch of white pepper. Pour into flan and bake as directed.

Christmas Flan

Place 8 oz chopped, mixed, cooked chicken (or turkey) and ham in the bottom of the uncooked pastry flan. Whisk together 2 large eggs, ¼ pint (⅝ cup) cream, 1 teaspoon chopped chives (optional), ¼ teaspoon salt and a pinch of white pepper. Pour into flan and bake as directed. This flan is ideal for using up Christmas leftovers.

Crayfish and Asparagus Flan

Place 4 oz flaked cooked crayfish, mixed with a medium size can asparagus, well-drained, and cut into 1 inch lengths in the bottom of the uncooked pastry flan. Whisk together 1 large egg, ¼ pint (⅝ cup) cream, ¼ teaspoon salt and a pinch of white pepper. Pour into flan, sprinkle with 1 tablespoon grated Parmesan cheese and bake as directed.

Mushroom Flan

Gently fry 1 sliced onion and 6 oz sliced mushrooms in 1 oz (1 tablespoon) butter or margarine until soft. Stir in 1 oz (2 tablespoons) plain flour and ½ cup milk and stir over heat until mixture boils. Cool and stir in 1 beaten egg, 2 tablespoons cream, ¼ teaspoon salt and freshly ground black pepper. Pour into uncooked pastry flan and bake as directed.

Onion Flan

Place 4 onions, thinly sliced, gently fried until soft, in 2 oz (2 tablespoons) butter or margarine, and 2 rashers of streaky bacon, rinded, diced and fried in the remaining fat and drained, into the bottom of the uncooked pastry flan. Whisk together 2 eggs, ¼ pint (⅝ cup) cream and a pinch of white pepper. Pour into flan, sprinkle with 1 tablespoon grated Parmesan cheese and bake as directed.

Cheese and Onion Flan

Place 2 onions, finely chopped and gently fried in 1 oz (1 tablespoon) butter or margarine, in the bottom of the uncooked pastry flan. Whisk together 2 large eggs, ¼ pint (⅝ cup) cream, 4 oz grated Cheddar or Gruyere cheese, ¼ teaspoon mustard powder, ¼ teaspoon salt and a pinch of white pepper. Pour into flan and bake as directed.

Spinach Flan

Mix together 1 cup cooked, well drained spinach, 2 beaten eggs, ¼ pint (⅝ cup) cream, ½ teaspoon ground nutmeg, ¼ teaspoon salt and a pinch of freshly ground black pepper. Pour into uncooked pastry flan, sprinkle with 1 tablespoon grated Parmesan cheese and bake as directed.

Tomato Flan

Place 1 onion, thinly sliced, gently fried until soft in 1 tablespoon olive oil and drained, into the bottom of the uncooked pastry flan. Cover with 1½ lb tomatoes, skinned and thickly sliced, 1 small can anchovy fillets, well-drained and cut into small pieces and 12 stoned, chopped black olives. Sprinkle with 1 tablespoon chopped fresh basil or 1 teaspoon dried basil and 1 tablespoon grated Parmesan cheese. Bake as directed.

Removing edge of a flan tin from Cheese and onion flan

Shepherd's Pie

Serves 4-6

Cooking time: 1½ hours

Oven temperature: 375-400°F

1 onion, finely chopped
2 tablespoons oil or dripping
1 lb minced beef
1 cup water
1 beef stock cube
1 tablespoon tomato sauce
2 teaspoons Worcestershire sauce
1 teaspoon dried mixed herbs
1 tablespoon chopped parsley
salt and pepper
1½ lb potatoes
1 oz (1 tablespoon) butter or margarine
½ cup milk

This is a potato covered pie of old rural England.
Gently fry onion in heated oil or dripping until soft, add
beef and cook, stirring frequently, until it loses its red
colour. Add water, crumbled stock cube, sauces, herbs, salt
and pepper, cover and simmer for 45 minutes-1 hour.
Boil peeled potatoes in salted water, drain and mash well.
Add butter or margarine and milk and beat well until smooth.
Place meat mixture into a greased 2 pint (5 cup) pie dish.
Top with the creamed potatoes, spreading with a fork to
cover meat completely. Decorate potato with a fork. Place
on a baking tray and bake in a moderately hot oven for 30
minutes or until hot and golden brown. Serve hot with a
green vegetable.
*Storage tip: Shepherd's Pie may be prepared, without
baking, covered with foil or plastic wrap and refrigerated
overnight. Bake the next day.*

Beef Meat Loaf

Serves 6

Cooking time: 1 hour

Oven temperature: 375-400°F

1½ lb minced beef
1 x ½ inch slice of bread
¼ cup of milk
2 tablespoons Worcestershire sauce
¼ cup fruit chutney
1 stock cube, crumbled
1½ teaspoons salt
½ teaspoon pepper
1 stalk celery, finely chopped
1 rasher bacon, diced, optional

Ask your butcher for best quality minced beef.
Soak bread in milk for 10 minutes. Mix together with minced
beef and remaining ingredients. Place mixture in a greased
2 lb loaf tin, previously base-lined with a strip of aluminium
foil. Place in a moderately hot oven and cook for 1 hour.
Serve hot with creamed potatoes and a green vegetable. To
serve cold, cool for 1 hour in the loaf tin before removing.
Turn out onto a flat serving plate. Serve cold meat loaf in
slices with mixed salads.
*Storage tip: Store cold meat loaf, wrapped in aluminium foil,
in refrigerator, in hot climates, and remove 30 minutes before
serving. Cold meat loaf should be served at room temperature
for the best flavour. Reheat meat loaf in a moderate oven for
20-30 minutes if you want to serve it hot.*

Steak and Kidney Pie

Serves 4-6

Cooking time: 2 hours

Oven temperature: 400-450°F/325-350°F

8 oz flaky or rough puff pastry (see pages 50 and 51)
1½ lb stewing beef, skirt or topside
 8 oz ox kidney
½ oz (1 tablespoon) plain flour
½ teaspoon salt
¼ teaspoon white pepper
4 shallots (spring onions), thinly sliced
1 teaspoon chopped parsley (optional)
½ pint (1¼ cups) cold water
1 egg for glazing
½ pint (1¼ cups) beef stock, for serving

Prepare the pastry and chill in refrigerator until required.
Trim fat and tissues from beef, cut beef into 3 x 1½ inch
strips and beat with a cleaver, meat mallet or rolling pin to
tenderise.
Skin and core kidney, cut into small cubes. Place a cube of
kidney on each strip of beef, roll up tightly and roll in flour
mixed with salt and pepper.
Place in a 1½ - 2 pint (5 cup) pie dish, sprinkle with sliced
shallots and chopped parsley, if used. Place a pie funnel in
the centre of the meat if liked, to allow steam to escape
during baking, and add water.
Roll pastry out on a lightly floured board or surface, ¼ inch
thick and large enough to cover pie with a ½ inch border.
Cut ½ inch border from rolled pastry, damp rim of pie dish
with cold water, press strip of pastry on rim and brush with
cold water. Lift pastry up with rolling pin and unroll on to
pie. Ease pastry into shape without stretching and press firmly
on to pastry rim to seal well. Trim pastry to fit dish, holding
pie in one hand and holding knife at an angle away from
edge of dish and cutting with short, sharp strokes.
Knock up the edge of the pie to seal, using the blade of a
knife, and scallop edge. Make leaves or a rose or a thistle for
decoration from remaining scraps of pastry. Brush pie with
beaten egg, do not brush edges or this will prevent them
rising.
Place decoration on pie and brush with beaten egg. Place on
a baking tray and bake towards the top of a hot oven for 30
minutes to cook pastry, then cover pastry with a piece of
wet greaseproof paper, pleating and twisting it under the pie
dish, and continue cooking the pie in a moderately slow oven

Steak and kidney pie

for a further 1½ hours to cook the filling.

To serve, cut away a portion of pastry and dilute the thick gravy with some hot, strong beef stock. This may be poured through the pie funnel if desired. Serve hot with vegetables. The beef may be cut into 1 inch cubes, rolled in the seasoned flour with the kidney and placed in the pie dish instead of preparing in rolls as described in the recipe.

Storage tip: The pie may be precooked on the night before serving for the first 30 minutes at least, to cook the pastry, and for longer if desired. Allow the pie to cool then refrigerate overnight. Continue baking the pie the next night, or day, covered with a fresh piece of wet greaseproof paper, in a moderate oven (350-375°F.) for the remaining required time. The cooked pie freezes very well.

Rough Puff Pastry

Makes 8 oz

8 oz (2 cups) plain flour
pinch of salt
3 oz butter or hard margarine
3 oz lard
cold water to mix

Sift flour and salt into a mixing bowl. Cut the fat into even sized pieces the size of a walnut and drop into the flour, tossing each piece well to coat it with flour. Add sufficient cold water and mix quickly to a soft dough using a round bladed knife.

Roll the dough out to an oblong on a lightly floured surface, fold in three and make a half turn so that an open end faces you. Repeat the rolling, folding and turning process twice more. Refrigerate the dough at any stage when it becomes too soft and greasy to handle. Wrap in a plastic bag and refrigerate until required.

Roll out and bake according to particular recipe.

Storage tip: Rough puff pastry stores well for a few days in a plastic bag in the refrigerator. It also freezes well.

Flaky Pastry

Makes 8 oz

8 oz (2 cups) plain flour
pinch of salt
3 oz butter or hard margarine
3 oz lard
cold water to mix

Sift flour and salt into a mixing bowl. Mix the fats together
on a plate with a knife and shape into a square block. Rub a
quarter of the mixed fat into the flour and mix to a firm
dough with cold water, using a round bladed knife.
Knead the dough lightly until smooth, then roll out to an
oblong on a lightly floured surface. Put another quarter of
the mixed fat in small pieces on the top two-thirds of the
dough. Fold in three, folding the bottom third up and the top
third down. This gives you even layers of dough and fat. Half
turn the pastry, so that an open end faces you, and roll out
again to an oblong.
Repeat flaking, folding and rolling of dough twice more.
Refrigerate the dough at any stage when it becomes too soft
and greasy to handle. Fold pastry into three once more, wrap
in a plastic bag and refrigerate until required.
Roll out and bake according to particular recipe.
When a recipe quotes 8 oz flaky pastry, this means you use 8
oz flour, not the total weight of the dough.
*Storage tip: The flaky pastry will keep well for a few days in
the refrigerator in a plastic bag. It also freezes well.*

Chicken Pie

Serves 4-6

Cooking time: 1½ hours

Oven temperature: 400-450° F

8 oz flaky or rough puff pastry (see pages 50 and 51) or
  commercial puff pastry
1 x 3 lb chicken
1 onion, coarsely chopped
1 bouquet garni
8 oz mushrooms
2 oz (2 tablespoons) butter or margarine
1 oz (2 tablespoons) plain flour
1 cup chicken stock
1 tablespoon chopped parsley
salt and pepper
4 tablespoons cream
2 tablespoons white wine (optional)
1 egg, for glazing

Prepare the pastry and chill in refrigerator until required.
Place the chicken, dressed and trussed, into a large pan with
the onion, bouquet garni and sufficient cold water to cover.
Place a circle of greased, greaseproof paper on top of the
chicken, cover pan with a tight fitting lid, bring slowly to the
boil and simmer until chicken is tender; about 1 hour. The
paper helps to conserve the chicken's flavour during cooking.
Remove cooked chicken from stock and leave to cool.
Fry the mushrooms whole in the heated fat in a saucepan. Add
flour and stir over a medium heat for 1 minute. Add chicken
stock and bring to the boil, stirring continuously. Stir in
parsley, salt and pepper to taste, cream and wine, if used.
Take chicken meat off carcass, remove skin and cut chicken
meat into bite-sized pieces. Place in 2 pint (5 cups) pie dish
in layers, alternating with the mushroom sauce. Leave until
cold, then cover with pastry as directed in Steak and
Kidney Pie (see page 48). Brush pastry with beaten egg.
Place pie on a baking tray and bake towards the top of a
hot oven for 25-35 minutes, or until pastry is cooked and
well browned. Serve hot with vegetables.
*Storage tip: Store the cooked pie, when cool, in the
refrigerator overnight. Reheat the next day or night in a
moderate oven (350-375° F) for 30-40 minutes or until
hot, covered with a piece of wet greaseproof paper.*

*However, you will produce a better pie if you refrigerate
overnight, uncooked, and bake the following night.*

Veal and Ham Pie

Serves 4-6

Cooking time: 1½ hours

Oven temperature: 400-450° F/325-350° F

8 oz flaky or rough puff pastry (see pages 50 and 51) or
    commercial puff pastry
1½ lb stewing veal
4 oz lean, cooked ham
1 tablespoon finely chopped onion
1 tablespoon chopped parsley
finely grated rind of 1 lemon
½ teaspoon salt
¼ teaspoon white pepper
1 pint (2½ cups) chicken stock
1 egg, for glazing

Prepare the pastry and chill in refrigerator until required.
Trim veal and cut into 1½ inch cubes. Cut ham into cubes.
Place prepared veal, ham, onion, parsley and lemon rind in
2 pint (5 cups) pie dish in layers, seasoning each layer with
salt and pepper. Add sufficient stock to threequarters
fill the pie dish.
Roll pastry out and cover pie as directed in Steak and Kidney
Pie recipe (see page 48). Glaze pie with beaten egg and
decorate with pastry leaves or a pastry rose.
Place pie on a baking tray and bake towards the top of a hot
oven for 30 minutes to cook pastry, then cover pie with a
piece of wet greaseproof paper and continue cooking in
a moderately slow oven for a further 1 hour or until meat
is tender. Test meat with a skewer if necessary.
To serve, add some more hot stock through a hole in the
pastry crust. Serve hot with vegetables or cold with
salad.
Storage tip: As for Steak and Kidney Pie.

Rabbit Pie

Serves 4-6

Cooking time: 2½ hours

Oven temperature: 325-350° F/400-450° F

8 oz flaky or rough puff pastry (see pages 50 and 51) or
    commercial puff pastry
8 oz bacon, rinded and diced
1 oz lard or dripping
1 x 2lb rabbit, jointed
1½ oz (3 tablespoons) plain flour
¾ pint (approx. 2 cups) stock or water and stock cubes
4 oz mushrooms
1 oz (1 tablespoon) butter or margarine
salt and pepper
1 egg, for glazing

Prepare the pastry and chill in refrigerator until required.
Fry bacon in a heated frying pan (skillet) in its own fat.
Drain and place in a casserole. Heat lard or dripping in pan.
Coat rabbit joints with flour and fry on all sides until brown.
Place rabbit in casserole. Add any remaining flour to pan and
cook for 1-2 minutes until golden. Add stock, bring to boil
stirring continuously, then add to casserole. Cover and cook
in a moderately slow oven for 1½ hours or until rabbit is
tender. Leave to cool.
Remove meat from cold rabbit and place in a 2 pint (5 cups)
pie dish, discard bones. Fry mushrooms in butter or
margarine and add to rabbit. Pour the meat liquor over.
Season with salt and pepper.
Roll out pastry and cover and decorate pie as directed in
Steak and Kidney Pie (see page 48). Glaze pie with beaten
egg.
Place pie on a baking tray and bake towards the top of a hot
oven for 25-35 minutes or until pastry is cooked and golden
brown. Serve hot with vegetables.
*Storage tip: Store the cold pie in refrigerator and reheat next
day in a moderate oven for 30-45 minutes or until hot.
However, you will get a better result if you store the shaped
pie, covered, without baking, in the refrigerator overnight and
bake it fresh the next day.*

Casseroles

Basic Beef Casserole

Serves 4

Cooking time: 1½ - 2 hours

Oven temperature: 325-350° F

1½ lb stewing beef, chuck, blade or topside
1½ oz (3 tablespoons) plain flour
1 onion, chopped
1 oz dripping or oil or margarine
1 carrot, sliced
1 pint (2½ cups) water
1 beef stock cube
1 teaspoon salt
1 teaspoon black pepper

Remove fat and any coarse tissue from beef. Beat beef with
a cleaver, wooden meat mallet or rolling pin to break the
tissues and help make it tender. Toss beef with flour in a clean
plastic bag until well coated.
Gently fry onion in heated fat in a heavy based pan until
golden, transfer to a plate. Fry beef and flour in pan over a
medium-high heat, stirring occasionally, until browned on all
sides. Add carrot and return onions to pan. Add water,
crumbled stock cube, salt and pepper and bring to the boil,
stirring occasionally to loosen sediment on base of pan. Add
ingredients according to choice as directed in 'Variations'.
Transfer to a casserole, cover with a tight-fitting lid and cook
in a moderately slow oven for 1-1½ hours, or until beef is
tender.
If you possess a flameproof casserole, the casserole may be
prepared in this on top of the stove, instead of in a pan, and
transferred to the oven for casseroling.
If you do not possess a casserole, this dish can be stewed very
slowly on top of the stove in a heavy based pan covered with
a tight fitting lid.
*Storage tip: Allow casserole to cool, then store covered in
casserole in refrigerator in hot climates. In cold climates the
casserole may be placed in a cool, dry place overnight. This
allows the flavour to develop. All meat casseroles freeze well
provided they do not contain herbs and wine.*

Basic beef casserole with eight variations

Variations of Basic Beef Casserole

Australian Beef Casserole

Add 1 tablespoon each of Worcestershire sauce, tomato sauce, vinegar and brown sugar and ½ teaspoon ground nutmeg, before transferring to casserole. Serve hot with creamed potatoes or jacket baked potatoes and a green vegetable.

Belgian Beef Casserole

Use 1 pint (2½ cups) beer instead of water and stock cubes. Add 1 clove finely chopped garlic before transferring to casserole. Serve with boiled potatoes.

Chinese Beef Casserole

Use oil for frying instead of dripping. Add 2 tablespoons soy sauce, 8 oz green beans cut into 2 inch lengths, and 1 red pepper, seeded, cut into julienne (matchlike) strips and blanched in boiling water for 1 minute, 20 minutes before end of cooking time. Serve with boiled rice.

French Beef Casserole

Add 4 oz diced salt pork or bacon, 2 tablespoons tomato paste (purée) and a bouquet garni before transferring to casserole. Fry 8 small, whole pickling onions and 4 oz mushrooms in 1 oz dripping until golden brown and add 20 minutes before end of cooking time. Serve sprinkled with chopped parsley. Serve with new potatoes, boiled macaroni noodles or rice. Follow with a tossed green salad.

Hungarian Beef Casserole

Add 8 oz sliced carrots, 1 lb sliced potatoes, 1 tablespoon paprika pepper and 1 clove finely chopped garlic before transferring to casserole. Just before serving stir in 2 tablespoons sour cream. Serve with 2 extra tablespoons sour cream on top of each portion.

Indian Beef Casserole

Add 1 tablespoon curry powder to the flour before tossing the beef. Add 1 apple, peeled, cored and chopped and 2 tomatoes, peeled and chopped before transferring to casserole. Stir in 1 tablespoon each of lemon juice, fruit

58

chutney and marmalade or redcurrant jelly just before serving.
Serve garnished with lemon segments and parsley sprigs.
Serve with boiled rice, sliced banana in lemon juice and fruit
chutney.

Russian Beef Casserole

Use 3 sliced onions instead of 1 chopped onion as directed
in basic recipe. Add 4 tablespoons concentrated tomato paste
(puree), 4 oz sliced mushrooms and 1 clove finely chopped
garlic before transferring to casserole. Stir in 2 tablespoons
sour cream just before serving. Serve 2 extra tablespoons
sour cream on top. Serve with macaroni noodles and
cabbage or cole slaw salad.

English Beef Casserole

Add 1 small turnip, peeled and chopped and 2 stalks celery,
sliced, before transferring to casserole. Add 4 oz peas and
2 skinned, chopped tomatoes 20 minutes before end of
cooking time. Serve sprinkled with chopped parsley. Serve
with boiled or jacket baked potatoes.

Basic Lamb Casserole

Serves 4

Cooking time: 1½ - 2 hours

Oven temperature: 325-350° F

1½ lb stewing lamb or hogget (mutton)
2 onions, quartered
1 oz dripping, oil, butter or margarine
1½ oz (3 tablespoons) plain flour
1 pint (2½ cups) water
1 beef or chicken stock cube
1 teaspoon salt
¼ teaspoon white pepper

Remove excess fat from meat and cut meat into cubes or
serving portions, if chops or cutlets. Gently fry onions in
heated fat in a heavy based pan until golden. Add meat and
fry until brown on all sides. Sprinkle flour over meat, stir and
cook gently for 1 minute until the roux is golden. Add water,
crumbled stock cube, salt and pepper and bring to the boil,
stirring occasionally to loosen sediment on base of pan.
Add ingredients according to choice as directed in
'Variations'. Transfer to casserole, cover with a tight fitting
lid and cook in a moderately slow oven for 1-1½ hours, or
until meat is tender.
Storage tip: As for Basic Beef Casserole.

Variations of Basic Lamb Casserole

French Lamb Casserole

Add 4 tablespoons concentrated tomato paste (purée),
1 clove finely chopped garlic and a bouquet garni before
transferring to casserole. Fry 8 small, whole pickling onions
in 1 oz butter or margarine until golden brown and add along
with ½ cup green peas, 20 minutes before end of cooking
time. Serve sprinkled with chopped parsley. Serve with
creamed potatoes or new potatoes.

Greek Lamb Casserole

Add 2 tablespoons concentrated tomato paste or 2 tomatoes,

60   French lamb casserole

peeled and chopped, ½ eggplant (aubergine), peeled and diced, 4 sliced zucchini (courgette) and the finely grated rind and juice of 1 lemon, before transferring to casserole. Serve with boiled rice.

Indian Lamb Casserole

Sprinkle 1 tablespoon curry powder over meat with flour. Add 1 clove finely chopped garlic, ¼ teaspoon ground ginger, 2 stalks chopped celery and 2 tablespoons sultanas before transferring to casserole. Stir in 4 tablespoons plain yoghurt just before serving. Serve with boiled rice and mango chutney.

Irish Lamb Casserole

Add 2 extra onions to basic recipe. Add 8 oz rinded, chopped bacon, before transferring to casserole and cover with 1 lb thinly sliced potatoes. Remove casserole lid for last 30 minutes to brown potatoes. Serve sprinkled with chopped parsley.

Italian Lamb Casserole

Add 1 medium size can Italian plum tomatoes, 1 clove finely chopped garlic and ½ teaspoon each dried basil and oregano or 1 tablespoon each chopped fresh basil and oregano, before transferring to casserole. Serve sprinkled with grated Parmesan cheese accompanied with boiled macaroni noodles or rice.

Australian Lamb Casserole

Add 1 sliced carrot, 1 small turnip and 8 oz pumpkin cut into chunky pieces and 1 teaspoon dried rosemary or 1 tablespoon chopped fresh rosemary, before transferring to casserole. Serve sprinkled with chopped parsley. Serve with creamed potatoes and a green vegetable.

Scottish Lamb Casserole

Add 2 tablespoons haricot beans, previously soaked in cold water overnight, or for 8 hours, 1 sliced carrot and 1 sliced turnip, before transferring to casserole. Serve with plain boiled potatoes.

Spanish Lamb Casserole

Add 2 seeded and sliced red or green peppers (capsicums), before transferring to casserole. Just before serving, stir in 2 tablespoons dry sherry and 12 stoned, sliced olives and heat through gently. Serve with boiled rice.

Basic Pork Casserole

Serves 4

Cooking time: 1½-2 hours

Oven temperature: 325-350°F

1½ lb lean stewing pork
1 onion, sliced
1 oz butter or margarine
1½ oz (3 tablespoons) plain flour
1 pint (2½ cups) water
1 chicken stock cube
1 teaspoon salt
¼ teaspoon white pepper

Remove fat from pork and cut pork into 1 inch cubes. Gently
fry sliced onion in heated fat in a heavy based pan until soft
and golden. Add pork and fry until golden brown on all sides,
stirring occasionally. Sprinkle flour over pork, stir and cook
gently for 1 minute until roux is golden. Add water, crumbled
stock cube, salt and pepper and bring to the boil, stirring
occasionally to loosen sediment on base of pan. Add
ingredients according to choice as directed in 'Variations'.
Transfer to a casserole, cover with a tight fitting lid and
cook in a moderately slow oven for 1-1½ hours, or until
pork is tender.
Storage tip: As for Basic Beef Casserole.

Variations of Basic Pork Casserole

American Pork Casserole
Add 1 medium size can baked beans or red kidney beans
and 4 rashers bacon, rinded and cut into 1 inch strips,
before transferring to casserole. Serve with boiled
potatoes.

Belgian Pork Casserole

Add ½ pint (1¼ cups) red wine in place of ½ pint water. Add 8 oz prunes before transferring to casserole. Stir in 1 tablespoon redcurrant jelly before serving. Serve sprinkled with chopped parsley.

Chinese Pork Casserole

Use oil for frying instead of butter. Add 2 tablespoons each of brown sugar, tomato sauce, vinegar and soy sauce before transferring to casserole. Add 1 carrot, cut in julienne (matchlike) strips, 1 green pepper, seeded, cut in julienne strips and blanched for 1 minute in boiling water and 1 cup pineapple cubes (fresh preferably) 15-20 minutes before cooking time is completed. If using canned pineapple, omit brown sugar. Serve with boiled rice.

English Pork Casserole

Use ½ pint (1¼ cups) water only and make up to 1 pint with cider. Add 1 teaspoon dried sage or 1 tablespoon chopped fresh sage and 2 peeled, cored and sliced apples 30 minutes before cooking time is completed. You may like to try adding 1 sliced pig's kidney to the pork for a rich flavour. Serve with creamed potatoes and a green vegetable.

French Pork Casserole

Add 8 oz sliced mushrooms and 1 clove finely chopped garlic before transferring to casserole. Just before serving, stir in 2 tablespoons each of brandy and cream and heat through gently without boiling. Serve sprinkled with chopped parsley. Serve with new potatoes or egg noodles. Follow with a tossed green salad.

German Pork Casserole

Add 8 oz Frankfurts, cut into 1 inch pieces, 1 cup drained sauerkraut, ½ teaspoon caraway seeds and 1 teaspoon German mustard 15-20 minutes before cooking time is completed. Serve with boiled or sautéed potatoes.

Hungarian Pork Casserole

Add 8 oz sliced carrots, 1 lb sliced potatoes, 2 peeled, quartered tomatoes and 1 tablespoon paprika pepper before transferring to casserole. Just before serving add 2 tablespoons sour cream.

Scandinavian Pork Casserole

Use lard for frying instead of butter or margarine. Add 2 chopped apples and 8 oz diced, cooked ham 15 minutes before cooking time is completed. Just before serving, stir in 4 tablespoons cream and heat through, without boiling. Serve with red cabbage and sauteed potatoes.

Boeuf Bourguignonne

Serves 12

Cooking time: 2¼-2¾ hours

Oven temperature: 300-325°F

4 lb topside (round) or rump (sirloin) steak
2 oz (4 tablespoons) plain flour
4 tablespoons olive oil
4 oz (4 tablespoons) butter or margarine
8 oz bacon or pork, diced
6 tablespoons brandy (optional)
4 carrots, chopped
2 leeks, sliced
2 onions, chopped
2 cloves garlic, crushed
1 bouquet garni
4 teaspoons salt
freshly ground black pepper
1 pint (2½ cups) Burgundy
1 pint (2½ cups) beef stock or water and beef stock cube
2 tablespoons cornflour
24 button onions
24 button mushrooms
extra oil and butter for frying
juice of 1 large lemon
chopped parsley for garnish

Cut beef into 2 inch cubes and roll in flour. Heat oil and
butter in a large heavy pan, or frying pan or skillet and
fry bacon or pork until crisp, transfer to a large casserole.
Fry meat in two or three parts until it changes colour on
all sides. Add heated brandy, if used, to last part of meat and
ignite. Let flame burn away and transfer all meat and juices
to casserole. Add carrots, leeks, onions and garlic to pan and
fry until golden then add to casserole. Add bouquet garni,
salt, pepper and Burgundy to casserole. Add stock to pan and
heat, stirring continuously to loosen meat sediment, then add
to casserole.
Cover and cook in a slow oven for 1½-2 hours.
Blend cornflour with 2 tablespoons cold water to a smooth
paste. Add to casserole and bring back to boiling point,
stirring occasionally.

Saute button onions and mushrooms in extra oil and butter,
add lemon juice and simmer till tender. Add to casserole and
serve hot sprinkled with chopped parsley.

Boeuf Bourguignonne is usually thickened with a 'beurre manie'
a butter and flour paste - but it is more successful to thicken
a large quantity with blended cornflour. Allow 1 lb meat for
3-4 people in this type of casserole dish.

*Storage tip: This dish may be cooked completely the night
before, cooled, covered and stored in the refrigerator and
reheated the next day or night for serving. This kind of
casserole improves in flavour on standing overnight.*

Chicken Curry

Serves 4

Cooking time: 1¾ hours

Oven temperature: 325-350° F

2 x 1lb chicken breasts
1 teaspoon ground turmeric
1 teaspoon ground cummin
1 clove garlic, crushed
1½ x 8 oz cartons plain yoghurt
1 oz (1 tablespoon) butter or margarine
1 onion, sliced
¼ teaspoon ground cloves
1 teaspoon ground cinnamon
salt

Remove skin and bone from chicken breasts and cut into bite
size pieces. Blend turmeric, cummin and crushed garlic with 1
carton yoghurt. Marinate chicken in yoghurt mixture for 1
hour.

Heat butter or margarine and gently fry sliced onion in a
flameproof casserole until soft without browning. Add spices,
fry for a few minutes, then add meat and marinade. Add a
little salt.

Cover and cook in a moderately slow oven for 1½ hours, or
until tender. Stir in extra yoghurt just before serving. This is a
mild but spicy curry. Serve hot with boiled rice.

*Storage tip: Cool and store covered overnight in a refrigerator
or in a cold place. The flavour of a curry develops with standing.*

Swiss Veal

Serves 8

Cooking time: 45 minutes-1 hour

Oven temperature: 350-375°F

3 lb boned leg of veal (schnitzel veal)
3 oz (6 tablespoons) plain flour
salt and pepper
6 oz (6 tablespoons) butter or margarine
2 onions, finely chopped
1½ cups dry white wine
8-12 oz mushrooms, chopped
1½ cups cream
1 tablespoon chopped parsley
¼ teaspoon paprika pepper

Cut veal into narrow strips 2 inches long and ¼ inch thick.
Mix the flour with salt and pepper and dip the veal into the
seasoned flour. Heat 4 oz butter or margarine in a frying pan
or skillet and fry the veal and chopped onion until lightly
browned, stirring occasionally. Add the wine and cook over
a medium heat stirring to a smooth consistency.
Fry the chopped mushrooms in the remaining butter or
margarine for 5 minutes. Stir in cream, parsley and paprika
pepper.
Mix the veal mixture gently with the mushroom mixture in
a casserole and season to taste with salt and pepper. Reheat in
a moderate oven without allowing it to boil. Serve hot with
noodles or sautéed potatoes, and green salad.
*Storage tip: Allow to cool after combining veal and
mushroom mixture, cover and refrigerate overnight. Heat
through in a moderate oven just before serving.*

Swiss veal for a formal dinner party

Lamb Curry

Serves 6-8

Cooking time: 2 hours

8 oz dried apricots
2 lb boneless shoulder of lamb
2 oz (2 tablespoons) butter or margarine
4 onions, chopped
2 teaspoons ground coriander
2 teaspoons ground cummin
1 teaspoon ground cinnamon
salt and pepper

Soak apricots in 1 pint (2½ cups) boiling water for 1-2 hours.
Trim fat from meat and cut into 1 inch pieces. Heat butter or margarine in a heavy based pan and fry onions until soft and golden, stirring continuously. Add the lamb, increase heat and cook until browned all over. Add spices and fry, stirring for 2-3 minutes. Add apricots and water in which they were soaked. Season with salt and pepper.
Cover, bring to the boil gently and simmer for 1½ hours, or until tender, stirring occasionally. Serve hot with boiled rice.
Storage tip: Cool and store covered in refrigerator or in a cold place overnight. Reheat next day.

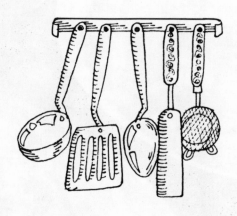

Blanquette of Veal

Serves 8

Cooking time: 1½ hours

2 lb boneless shoulder of veal
1 lb boneless breast of veal
2 onions
2 carrots
1 bouquet garni
salt and pepper
1½ pints (approx 4 cups) water
1½ oz (1½ tablespoons) butter or margarine
1½ oz (3 tablespoons) plain flour
2 egg yolks
¼ pint ($^2/_3$ cup) milk or cream
lemon juice to taste
chopped parsley for garnish

Cut veal into chunky 2 inch pieces. Place in a large heavy
based pan with onions and carrots previously cut into
quarters. Add bouquet garni, salt and pepper and water. Cover
and simmer very gently for 1 hour or until veal is tender.
Pour liquor from pan. Measure liquor and boil to reduce to 1
pint (2½ cups) if necessary.
Make a sauce by melting butter or margarine in a saucepan,
stir in flour and cook over a medium heat for a few seconds.
Add reduced stock and bring to the boil, stirring continuously.
Simmer for 1-2 minutes then draw aside.
Store veal and sauce overnight at this stage. Put veal and
vegetables into a bowl, cover and refrigerate when cool. Pour
sauce into a bowl, cover with a wet circle of greaseproof
paper and store in refrigerator.
When ready to serve next day, reheat sauce and veal in
separate pans. Blend egg yolks smoothly with milk or
cream and stir slowly into hot sauce. Add lemon juice and
seasoning to taste. Pour sauce over veal and shake pan gently
over heat to mix together. Cover and keep hot without boiling
for 10-15 minutes so that flavour of sauce penetrates veal.
Serve hot with creamed potatoes or boiled rice and a green
vegetable.
Storage tip: As given in recipe.

Coq Au Vin

Serves 8

Cooking time: 1½ hours

Oven temperature: 325-350°F

2 x 2 lb roasting chickens
2 oz (2 tablespoons) butter or margarine
2 tablespoons olive oil
4 rashers bacon, rinded
8 small pickling onions
2 tablespoons cognac or high proof brandy
½ bottle (1½ cups) Burgundy
½ pint (1¼ cups) chicken stock or water and chicken stock cube
2 cloves garlic, crushed
1 bouquet garni
salt and pepper
4 extra teaspoons butter
2 teaspoons plain flour
croutes of fried bread for serving
chopped parsley for garnish

Cut chicken into neat joints and brown slowly in heated butter
or margarine and oil in a flameproof casserole. Remove
from casserole. Cut bacon into strips and brown bacon and
onions in casserole. Return chicken to casserole, add cognac
and set alight. Keep lid close by in case flame leaps up. Pour
in wine and stock and add garlic, bouquet garni, salt and
pepper. Cover and cook in a moderately slow oven or
simmer gently on top of stove for 1 hour or until tender.
Blend extra butter to a smooth paste with flour and add to
casserole in small pieces, stirring occasionally to thicken
sauce. Season to taste. Serve hot surrounded by croûtes of
fried bread and sprinkle with chopped parsley. Use
French bread for croûtes to be authentic. Serve with
creamed or new potatoes.
*Storage tip: May be stored, covered, when cold, in refrigerator
overnight. Reheat and thicken as directed next day. This does
not freeze well.*

Desserts and Puddings

Charlotte Malakhov

Serves 8

8 sponge fingers (savoyardi)
2 tablespoons sherry or orange juice
4 oz unsalted butter or soft margarine
6 oz (¾ cup) castor sugar
few drops almond essence
3 egg yolks
6 oz (1½ cups) ground almonds
1 cup thickened cream

Line the bottom of a charlotte mould, or a round 6 inch
cake tin, with a piece of greaseproof paper or aluminium
foil. Place the sponge fingers around the sides of the
charlotte mould and pour the sherry over them.
Beat the butter or margarine, castor sugar and almond essence
together in a mixing bowl, until soft and creamy. Beat in egg
yolks gradually, then beat in ground almonds. Gradually add
three quarters of the cream, beating the mixture until it is
well blended. Place the mixture in the sponge lined mould and
level the surface. Trim sponge fingers level with mixture.
Cover with foil or clear plastic wrap and chill in the
refrigerator for 24 hours or until firm.
Turn Malakhov out onto a serving plate, tie a ribbon around
the sponge fingers if desired. Whip the remaining cream and
swirl or pipe on top of the dessert. Serve, cut in thin wedges,
with a bowl of sliced fresh strawberries.
*Storage tip: This should stand overnight in the refrigerator
to set, but it will also keep for a few days in the refrigerator.*

Chocolate Refrigerator Cake

Serves 8

Cooking time: 15 minutes

1 sponge cake
4 oz dark cooking chocolate
4 tablespoons milk
3 oz (3 tablespoons) sugar
4 egg yolks
1 teaspoon vanilla essence or liqueur
½ pint (1¼ cups) cream
extra 1 oz dark chocolate, grated, for decoration

Line a round 6 inch cake tin with foil or greaseproof paper
and cover the bottom and sides with thin slices of sponge
cake.
Melt chocolate in a heatproof bowl over hot water, stir in
milk.
Whisk sugar and egg yolks in a double boiler over hot water
until thick and creamy. Add chocolate mixture and cook
until mixture thickens. Add vanilla or liqueur.
Fill the tin with alternate layers of chocolate mixture and
slices of sponge cake, finishing with a layer of sponge cake.
Cover with foil or clear plastic wrap and chill overnight in
refrigerator or for 12 hours.
Turn out and cover with whipped cream, sprinkle with grated
chocolate.
Storage tip: As directed in recipe.

Water Ice

Serves 6 - 8

Cooking time: 5 minutes

1 pint (2½ cups) water
8 oz (1 cup) sugar
½ pint (1¼ cups) lemon or orange juice
1 egg white

Place water and sugar in a clean pan and heat over a medium heat until the sugar dissolves. Simmer gently for 3 minutes, leave to cool.
Stir in lemon or orange juice, pour into an ice tray and freeze until soft and mushy, about 1-2 hours.
Fold in whisked egg white until texture is smooth and return to ice tray and freeze for 2-3 hours or overnight.
To serve, the water ice should be a soft mushy texture. If it is frozen hard, allow to stand at room temperature until it softens a little. Serve in glass dishes or in hollow oranges or lemons.
Variations: Sprinkle water ice with a little liqueur before serving.
To make a fruit water ice, use ½ pint (1¼ cups) water, 4 oz sugar and 1 pint (2½ cups) fresh fruit purée such as crushed strawberries, 1 aspberries, blackberries, apricots or mangoes and 1 egg white. To make a coffee water ice, use same proportions as for fruit water ice but substitute 1 pint strong black coffee for crushed fruit.
Storage tip: Make and store overnight in freezer.

Water ice (orange flavoured)

Gooseberry/Rhubarb Fool

Serves 6-8

Cooking time: 20 minutes

1 lb gooseberries or rhubarb
2-3 tablespoons sugar
3 tablespoons water
½ pint (1¼ cups) custard or
  ¼ pint ($^2/_3$ cup) custard and ¼ pint ($^2/_3$ cup) cream

Top and tail gooseberries or cut rhubarb into 1 inch pieces,
place in a pan with sugar and water, cover and stew till
tender. Cool fruit then sieve or mix to a purée in an electric
blender. Add custard, or custard and whipped cream, to fruit
purée.
Mix together and serve either in a large glass bowl or in
individual sundae glasses.
Quick tip: For a quality flavour, make a home-made pouring
custard with ½ pint (1¼ cups) milk, 1 egg or 2 egg yolks and
1 tablespoon sugar, but for convenience, make up ½ pint
(1¼ cups) custard with commercial custard powder.
*Storage tip: Cover fruit fool, in serving bowl or sundae
glasses, with clear plastic wrap and refrigerate overnight. You
can refrigerate the prepared fruit fool in a plastic air tight
container if you prefer and pour into serving bowl next
day before serving.*

Oranges in Kirsch

Serves 8

Cooking time: 10-15 minutes

8 oranges
8 tablespoons kirsch
Caramel:
4 oz (½ cup) sugar

Peel oranges with a sharp serrated knife. Take care to remove
all pith neatly. Cut oranges into thin slices, standing on a
plate in order to retain juice. Reshape oranges and secure with
wooden toothpicks. Place oranges, juice and kirsch in a plastic
container, seal well and macerate in refrigerator overnight.
Serve oranges, chilled, sprinkled with 'chopped' pieces of
caramel. Pour extra kirsch over just before serving if desired.

To make caramel: Place sugar in a heavy based pan, frying pan or skillet, heat slowly over a low heat until it forms a caramel.

Pour caramel quickly onto a sheet of greased greaseproof paper or aluminium foil, spread thinly and leave to set. When set, chop caramel with a sharp, French chopping knife and sprinkle over oranges before serving.

Storage tip: An airtight plastic container is ideal for storing the Oranges in Kirsch overnight, in the refrigerator, for no flavour is lost.

Blackberry and Apple Pie

Serves 6-8

Cooking time: 30-40 minutes

Oven temperature: 400-450°F

8 oz rich short crust pastry (see page 91)
1 lb cooking apples
1 box blackberries
2 tablespoons sugar
¼ teaspoon ground cinnamon (optional)
castor sugar for sprinkling

Roll out half the pastry into a round and line an 8-9 inch pie plate.

Peel, core and slice the apples. Pick the blackberries clean. Place apple and blackberries into pie plate, sprinkle with sugar and cinnamon, if desired. Brush edge of pastry with cold water. Roll out remaining pastry to a round, to fit pie plate and place on top of fruit. Seal edges, trim neatly, and decorate edge. Make a neat hole in the centre of pastry with a skewer to allow steam to escape.

Sprinkle pastry with a little castor sugar and bake towards the top of a hot oven for 30-40 minutes, until pastry is cooked and golden brown. Serve hot or cold with pouring custard or cream.

Variation: To ring the changes, use 1½ lb of apples, gooseberries, raspberries, cherries or apricots in the pie.

Storage tip: Allow to cool, cover with foil or clear plastic wrap and store in a cold place overnight (in refrigerator if the weather is hot). Reheat pie in a moderate oven (350-375°F) for 20-30 minutes before serving.

Pears in Red Wine

Serves 6

Cooking time: 35-40 minutes

Oven temperature: 350-375°F

6 oz (¾ cup) sugar
¼ pint (⅔cup) water
¼ pint (⅔cup) red wine
2 strips lemon rind
1 stick cinnamon or ¼ teaspoon ground cinnamon
6 ripe dessert pears
1 teaspoon arrowroot
1 tablespoon slivered almonds

Place sugar and water in a clean pan, heat gently until sugar
dissolves.
Add wine, lemon rind and cinnamon, bring to the boil, covered,
and boil for 1 minute.
Peel pears but leave the stalks on. Cut a thin slice off the
bottom so that they stand upright.
Place pears in a clean casserole, pour syrup-wine mixture over,
cover and stew gently in a moderate oven for 30-40 minutes
until tender but not mushy. Baste frequently while cooking.
Remove pears and stand upright in a serving dish.
Strain liquid into saucepan, cool slightly. Blend arrowroot
with a little cool liquid, stir into liquid in pan and bring to
the boil stirring continuously.
Pour over pears and sprinkle with almonds. Serve hot or
cold.
*Storage tip: Cool pears in serving bowl, cover with clear plastic
wrap and refrigerate overnight. Serve next day at room
temperature.*

Dutch Apple Flan

Serves 8-12

Cooking time: 30-40 minutes

Oven temperature: 400-425° F

Pastry:
6 oz (1½ cups) plain flour
1 teaspoon baking powder
3 oz margarine or butter
1 small egg
3 oz (3 tablespoons) castor sugar
1 teaspoon vanilla essence
Filling:
½ cup golden syrup
1 large egg
3 large cooking apples
2 oz dates, chopped
1 oz butter or margarine
cream or custard for serving

Pastry: Sift flour and baking powder into mixing bowl. Add
margarine, egg, sugar and vanilla essence and knead and
squeeze together to form a soft dough, using a clean hand (as
when making shortbread).
Roll out pastry to a rectangle and line a greased, shallow
12 x 8 inch cake tin (lamington tin), covering the bottom and
½ inch up the sides.
Filling: Gently heat the measured golden syrup and beat the
egg in off the heat.
Peel, core and slice apples into thin segments.
Pour half mixture over pastry and spread to edges. Cover
with neat rows of overlapping apple slices and pour remaining
syrup mixture over.
Sprinkle with chopped dates and dot with butter or margarine.
Bake towards the top of a hot oven for 30-40 minutes until
cooked. Serve warm, cut into squares, with whipped cream
or pouring custard.
*Storage tip: Cool flan, cover with foil and refrigerate overnight.
Reheat next day in a moderate oven for 30 minutes.*

82

Basic Fruit Flan

Serves 8

Cooking time: 30 minutes

Oven temperate: 375-400° F

4 oz rich short crust pastry (see page 91)
1 large can fruit or mixture of fruits
1 teaspoon arrowroot

This quantity, 4 oz rich short crust pastry, refers to the
measurement of flour in the recipe, so it actually weighs
6-7 oz when made up.
Roll out pastry on a lightly floured surface to a round, ⅛ inch
thick, large enough to line the bottom and sides of an 8-inch
flan tin or flan ring.
Lift pastry up with rolling pin and unroll over flan tin, or
flan ring, standing on a baking tray. Press pastry quickly into
shape, from the centre to the edge, with the back of a cold
hand. Roll pin lightly over edge to trim off excess pastry.
Prick base lightly with a fork and bake blind as directed.
To bake 'blind': Place a circle of greased, greaseproof paper
into pastry flan (greased side next to pastry) and cover base
with dried haricot beans or peas. Bake flan blind towards the
top of a moderately hot oven (375-400° F) for 15 minutes,
or until pastry is set in shape. Remove 'baking beans' and
greaseproof paper and continue baking for a further 10-15
minutes, or until pastry is cooked and golden. Remove flan
ring and slide flan onto a wire cooling tray. If baking in a flan
tin, remove from tin after a few minutes and cool on a wire
cooling tray.
To finish flan: Drain fruit and reserve ¼ pint (²/₃ cup) juice.
Arrange fruit attractively in cold pastry flan case.
Blend arrowroot with reserved juice in a small saucepan.
Bring to the boil, stirring continuously with a wooden spoon
until the mixture thickens and becomes clear. Pour slowly or
brush carefully over all the fruit in the flan and leave until set.
Decorate with rosettes of whipped cream if desired.
*Storage tip: The flan case may be made the night before,
cooled and stored in a cake tin overnight and filled with fruit
and glazed the next day.*

Cherry Compôte

Serves 6-8

Cooking time: 15 minutes

1½ lb dark red cherries
½ cup red wine or dry sherry
3 tablespoons redcurrant or grape jelly (conserve)
1 tablespoon sugar
grated rind and juice of 1 orange
pinch of ground cinnamon
1 tablespoon arrowroot or cornflour
2 tablespoons cold water

Stone cherries with a cherry stoner or the point of a vegetable peeler.

Place red wine, redcurrant jelly, sugar, orange rind, juice and cinnamon into a pan. Cover and heat gently until jelly is melted. Add cherries, cover and simmer for 5 minutes.

Blend arrowroot to a smooth paste with cold water. Stir into the cherries and bring to the boil, stirring continuously.

Cool and serve at room temperature for best natural flavour. It looks good in a polished glass bowl.

Variations: Use apricots or plums or greengages instead of cherries, but simmer for 15 minutes instead of 5 minutes.

Storage tip: Store cooled cômpote overnight in an airtight plastic container in refrigerator. Remove next day 1 hour before serving.

Cherry compôte

Peach Cobbler

Serves 8-12

Cooking time: 30 minutes

Oven temperature: 350-375° F

Pastry:
4 oz butter or margarine
2 oz (¼ cup) castor sugar
2 eggs
8 oz (2 cups) plain flour
1 teaspoon cream of tartar
¼ teaspoon bicarbonate of soda
pinch of salt
¼ pint (⅔cup) milk
Filling:
3 tablespoons tapioca, soaked overnight
3 oz butter or margarine
4 oz (½ cup) sugar
1 large can or 2 cups fresh sliced peaches
cream or custard for serving

Pastry: Cream the butter or margarine with sugar until light
and fluffy, add beaten eggs gradually, beating after each
addition. Sift flour, cream of tartar, bicarbonate of soda and
salt and mix to a dough along with the milk.
Knead lightly and press half pastry into shallow 12 x 8 inch
cake (lamington) tin.
Filling: Drain tapioca, place in a small heavy based pan, add
butter or margarine and sugar, cover and simmer gently until
tapioca is tender. Cool.
Pour the filling into the Pastry: case and arrange
sliced peaches on top.
Roll out remaining pastry on a lightly floured surface and place
on top of peaches.
Bake towards the top of a moderate oven for 30 minutes or
until pastry is cooked and golden. Serve warm, cut into
squares with whipped cream or pouring custard.
*Storage tip: Cool cobbler, cover with foil and refrigerate
overnight. Reheat next day in a moderate oven for 30-40
minutes.*

Strawberry Flan

Serves 12

Cooking time: 40 minutes

Oven temperature: 375-400° F/300-325° F

8 oz rich short crust pastry (see page 91) or 12 oz
   commercial short crust pastry
½ pint thickened cream
4 - 6 boxes strawberries (depending on size)
6 tablespoons redcurrant jelly
2 teaspoons cornflour
1 tablespoon cold water
juice of ½-1 orange

To make flan case: Roll out pastry to a circle ⅛ inch thick and
large enough to line a 12 inch flan ring standing on a baking
tray or a 12 inch flan tin.
Lift pastry onto rolling pin and unroll into flan tin. Trim as
for Basic Fruit Flan (see page 83). Prick pastry base and place a
large circle of greased greaseproof paper into flan with
greased side next to pastry. Fill with a layer of haricot beans.
This is known as a 'blind filling'.
Bake 'blind' on the centre shelf of a moderately hot oven
for 30 minutes, remove blind filling and bake for a further
10 minutes in a slow oven. Cool on a wire cooling tray a
few minutes before removing carefully from flan tin. Allow to
cool before filling.
To fill flan: Whip cream and spread evenly over base of flan.
Place hulled strawberries attractively on top.
Heat redcurrant jelly until melted and smooth. Blend cornflour
with cold water to a smooth paste. Stir into redcurrant jelly
and bring to the boil, stirring continuously until smooth. Stir
in sufficient orange juice to give a thin coating consistency.
Glaze strawberries, using a brush, while the glaze is still warm.
Allow to cool and set. Serve cut into segments.
*Storage tip: Store cold flan case in an air tight container
overnight and fill and glaze next day.*

French Apricot Tart

Serves 8

Cooking time: 20 minutes

Oven temperature: 400-450° F

Pastry:
6 oz (1½ cups) plain flour
pinch of salt
4 oz butter
1 tablespoon castor sugar
1 egg yolk
2 tablespoons water
Filling:
3 tablespoons custard powder
1 tablespoon sugar
½ pint (1¼ cups) milk
1 x 1 lb 13 oz can appricots, drained
apricot jam glaze
1 tablespoon browned almond slivers

Pastry: Sift flour and salt into a mixing bowl. Rub butter in with the fingertips until the mixture resembles breadcrumbs. Add sugar. Mix the egg yolk and water together and mix into the flour with a round bladed knife, until the mixture forms a soft dough. Chill for at least 30 minutes before rolling. Roll pastry out to a circle, ⅛ inch thick, and line an 8 inch flan ring. Bake blind (see page 83) towards the top of a hot oven for 20 minutes. Cool on a wire cooling tray.
Filling: Blend custard powder and sugar to a smooth paste with a little of the measured milk. Heat remaining milk, pour in blended custard powder and bring to the boil stirring continuously. Cool.
Put custard into pastry case, cover with the drained apricots, brush with apricot jam glaze and sprinkle almonds on top. Serve immediately.
Storage tip: Pastry case may be stored in a tin overnight. Custard may also be stored overnight in a covered container in the refrigerator. Finish flan just before serving.

Apricot tart

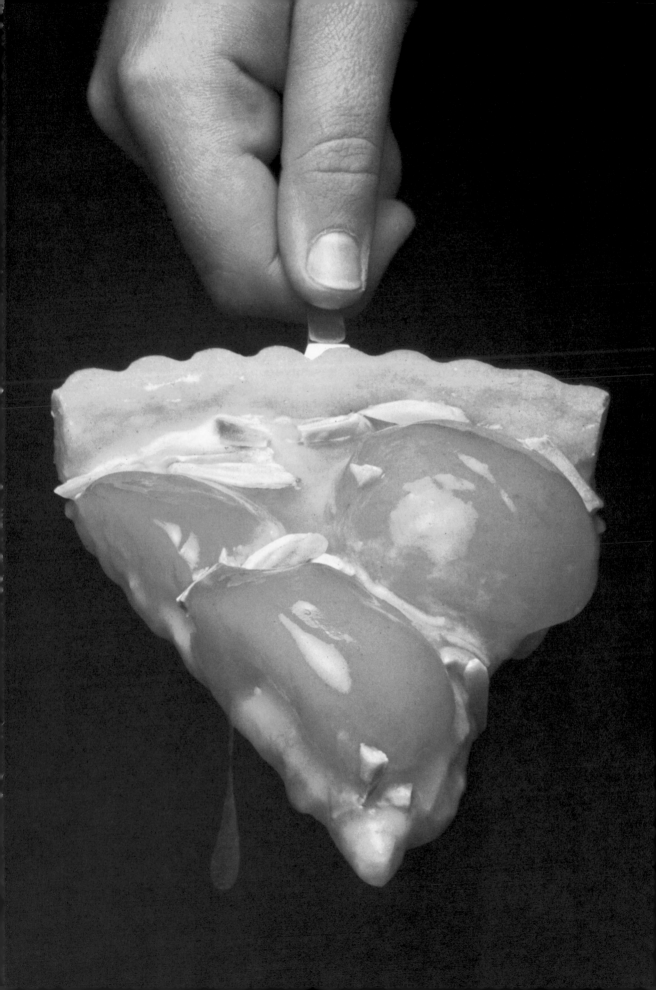

Liqueur Rum Truffles

Makes 18-24

3 oz cake crumbs
3 oz (3 tablespoons) castor sugar
3 oz ground almonds
1 teaspoon cocoa
1 tablespoon grated dark chocolate
1 egg yolk
1 tablespoon liqueur or rum
chocolate (vermicelli) sprinkles
small paper cases for serving

Place all dry ingredients in a mixing bowl and mix together. Stir
in egg yolk and 1 tablespoon of your favorite liqueur
(curaçao or grand marnier or tia maria are delicious) and mix
to a smooth paste.
Divide mixture into eighteen to twenty-four equal parts, as
desired, about a heaped teaspoon to each part, and roll gently
in cool, dry hands into a ball. Roll balls in chocolate
vermicelli, place in paper cases and refrigerate in a covered
plastic container until firm and set.
Serve as a petit four with coffee. These are very good to serve
at a buffet party, in place of a dessert, as they are so easy to
eat standing up.
*Storage tip: Store in an airtight plastic box in the refrigerator.
These will keep fresh for up to two weeks if stored this way.*